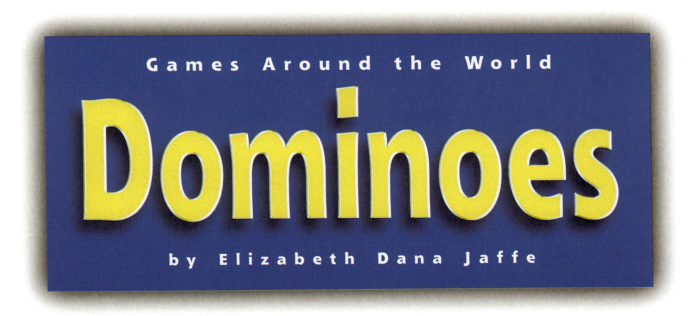

Games Around the World

Dominoes

by Elizabeth Dana Jaffe

Content Adviser: Professor Sherry L. Field, Department of Social Science Education, College of Education, The University of Georgia

Reading Adviser: Dr. Linda D. Labbo, Department of Reading Education, College of Education, The University of Georgia

COMPASS POINT BOOKS
MINNEAPOLIS, MINNESOTA

Compass Point Books
3722 West 50th Street, #115
Minneapolis, MN 55410

Visit Compass Point Books on the Internet at *www.compasspointbooks.com* or e-mail your
request to *custserv@compasspointbooks.com*

Photographs ©: Gregg Andersen, cover, 5, 11, 14; Owen Franken/Corbis, 4;
North Wind Picture Archives, 7; Stock Montage, 9; International Stock/Mitch
Diamond, 10; Photo Network/Buddy Jenssen, 12; TRIP/H. Rogers, 16; Unicorn
Stock Photos/Paul Murphy, 27.

Editors: E. Russell Primm and Emily J. Dolbear
Photo Researcher: Svetlana Zhurkina
Photo Selector: Linda S. Koutris
Designer: Bradfordesign, Inc.
Illustrator: Abby Bradford

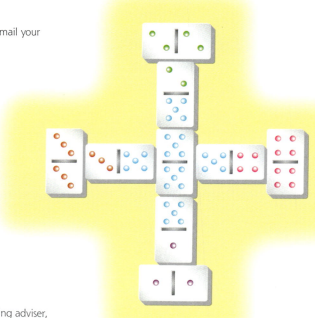

Library of Congress Cataloging-in-Publication Data

Jaffe, Elizabeth D.
    Dominoes / by Elizabeth Dana Jaffe ; content adviser, Sherry L. Field ; reading adviser,
Linda D. Labbo.
        p. cm. — (Games around the world)
    Includes bibliographical references and index.
    ISBN 0-7565-0132-6 (hardcover : lib. bdg.)
        1. Dominoes—Juvenile literature. [1. Dominoes.] I. Field, Sherry L. II. Labbo, Linda D. III. Title.
    GV1467 .J34 2002
    795.3'2—dc21
                                                                    2001001592

E795.32
JAF

Table of Contents

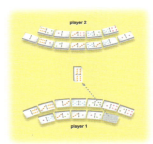

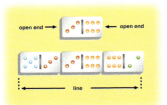

Click, Click, Click

Four people are playing a game at a table. Click, click, click. One person moves the game pieces all around. Click, click, click. The pieces are small white rectangles with black dots on them. Click, click, click. The time has come.

Each person takes seven game pieces. They begin putting the pieces down on the table. First, they **match** dots. Then they add the number of dots. They are playing **dominoes**!

They are having fun. You can learn to play dominoes too.

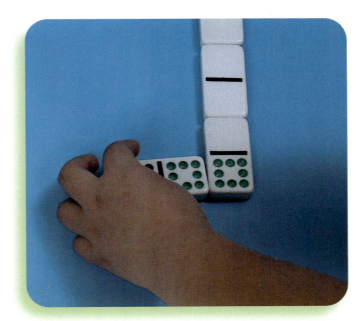

▲ *Matching dots in a game using a fifty-five-domino deck*

The History of Dominoes

Most people believe that the Chinese people invented dominoes. In 1120, the Chinese played a game like dominoes. Chinese dominoes were made of bone or ivory.

The Chinese play with twenty-one dominoes. A line divides each domino into two sections, or **ends**. All the dominoes have dots. That means there are no dominoes with a **blank** end.

Later, people in Europe played dominoes. They changed the game pieces. They made the dominoes shorter. They also added a blank end to the dominoes. In this way, the Europeans added seven dominoes to the Chinese game.

What Is a Double Zero?
The domino with two blank ends is called a double zero, a white, or a pale.

Playing dominoes in a café in Europe ▶

People used dominoes to play games, of course. They also used dominoes to teach children arithmetic. Bankers and traders used dominoes to help them count.

Italy was the first country in Europe to play a game with dominoes. In the early 1700s, the standard domino game spread to France. Then prisoners in France brought dominoes to England. The prisoners made their own dominoes.

Later, people in other parts of the world began to play dominoes. Today, dominoes are popular in Cuba, Spain, Vietnam, and the Ukraine. The Inuit in Alaska also play a kind of dominoes!

A young child playing with dominoes in the 1800s ▶

The Domino

Dominoes are often black or white rectangles. The dots on them are called **pips**. Dominoes are made of wood, ivory, or plastic. New domino sets come in many colors.

The side with pips on it is called the **face** of the domino. The side without pips is the back of the domino. Like a deck of cards, the backs of dominoes are all the same. They can be plain or decorated.

▲ *Dominoes come in many colors.*

◄ *The backs of these dominoes are decorated.*

In a standard set, twenty-one dominoes have pips on both ends. Seven dominoes have no pips on one end.

Today, a standard **deck** has twenty-eight dominoes. It is called the double six. That means the deck has a domino with six pips on both ends. There are also decks with fifty-five dominoes. That's called the double nine.

Dominoes are usually twice as long as they are wide. They are half as thick as they are wide. They are heavy enough to stand on their edges.

How Big Is a Domino?
A standard domino measures 1 by 2 by ½ inch (2.5 by 5 by 1.3 centimeters). Dominoes also come in bigger sizes for professional domino players.

◀ *A standard deck of twenty-eight dominoes*

How to Play Dominoes

To play dominoes, you need a flat surface and a set of dominoes. You spread out the dominoes—facedown—on a table. Then you mix them up. This pile of dominoes is called a **boneyard**.

Players **draw** dominoes from the boneyard. The dominoes they draw make up their **hands**. Players may or may not use the dominoes in the boneyard later in the game.

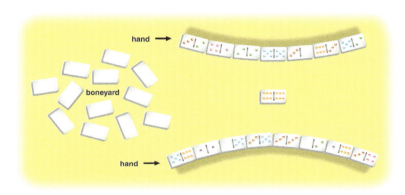

▲ *The player with the highest double goes first.*

Players stand each domino on its long edge. They make sure that the other players cannot see the faces of the dominoes. In most domino games, the object is to be the first player to get rid of all your dominoes.

The player with the highest **double** goes first. A double is a domino with the same number of pips at both ends.

◀ *The pile of dominoes is called the boneyard.*

If no one has a double, then the player who has the domino with the most pips goes first. The first player puts the domino faceup on the table. This first domino is called the **set**.

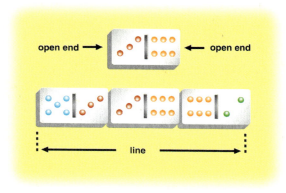

▲ *A line of play*

The person sitting to the left of the first player goes next. That player places his or her domino next to the end of the first domino with the same number of pips.

The first domino has two **open ends**. That means you can match the pips on your domino with either end of the first domino. As the game continues, a **line** forms.

Players add dominoes to the line in two ways. They can add a domino with the line or crosswise. Players usually place dominoes with the line.

Doubles are usually placed crosswise. You can play on both sides of a double. You can't play on the ends of a double.

◄ *A line of dominoes in play*

Block Dominoes—A Game from America

Many domino games around the world are based on block dominoes. In this game, after players draw their hands, they don't use the boneyard.

Number of players: Two to four

What you need: A twenty-eight-domino deck

Setup: Two players get eight dominoes each and three or four players get five dominoes each

Object: To be the first player to earn 100 points

How to play:

1. The first player puts down the set.

2. Each player then tries to match a domino in his or her hand with an open end on the line.

3. All doubles are placed crosswise. You cannot play on the ends of a double.

4. A player who can't match a domino misses a turn.

5. The first player to play all of his or her hand calls out "Domino!" and wins the round. The winner's score is the total number of pips in the other players' hands.

6. If no one has any dominoes left that match the open ends, the game is **blocked**. The winner of a blocked game is the player with the fewest pips on his or her dominoes. That player's score is the total number of the other players' pips minus his or her pips.

7. Continue playing rounds until someone earns 100 points.

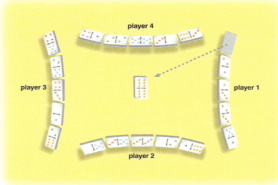

▲ *The first player puts down the set.*

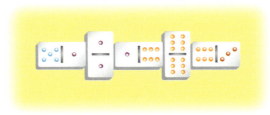

▲ *A line of play*

19

Draw Dominoes—A Game from America

This is the most common domino game. In this game, after players draw their hands, they can draw dominoes from the boneyard.

Number of players: Two to four

What you need: A twenty-eight-domino deck

Setup: Two players get eight dominoes each and three or four players get five dominoes each

Object: To be the first player to earn 100 points

How to play:

The rules are the same as block dominoes except:

1. When a player has no matching dominoes, the

player draws dominoes from the bone-yard until he or she can match a domino.

2. When a player draws from the boneyard, those dominoes become part of that player's hand.

3. If a player has no matching domino to play and there are no dominoes in the boneyard, the player misses a turn.

▲ *In draw dominoes, you can draw from the boneyard.*

Matador—A Game from Spain

In this game, you must match ends to equal seven. The zero domino and dominoes with seven pips are the "matadors." You can play matadors any time, but you must add them crosswise. You can draw from the boneyard.

Number of players:	Two to four
What you need:	A twenty-eight-domino deck
Setup:	Two players get eight dominoes, three players get six dominoes, and four players get five dominoes
Object:	To be the first player to earn 100 points
How to play:	
1.	The first player puts down the set.

2. The next player adds a domino so that the touching ends equal seven.

3. You get one point for each domino you play.

▲ *Matadors*

4. You must play all doubles, except the zero matador, with the line.

5. You can add on to a matador as long as your domino end and the pips on one

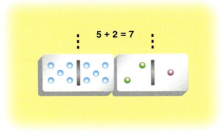

5 + 2 = 7

▲ *Touching ends must equal seven.*

What Is a Matador?

Many Spanish countries have bullfights. The bullfighter is called the *matador*.

23

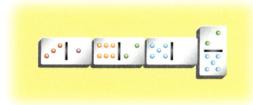

▲ *Matadors are played crosswise and at any time.*

▲ *When you add on to a matador, your domino end and the pips on one end of the matador must equal seven.*

end of the matador equal seven. If two matadors are played in a row, the second matador is played with the line.

6. If you can't play any of your dominoes, draw one from the boneyard. If you still can't play, you miss a turn. (You don't have to use your matadors.)

7. The first player to play all his or her hand calls "Domino!" and wins the round. The winner adds the points for each domino he or she played and the total pips in the other players' hands.

8. The round is also over if the game is blocked. To get your score, add the points for each domino you played and the total pips in the other players' hands. Then subtract the number of pips in your hand.

Hungarian Dominoes

This is a block game played in Hungary. Like block dominoes, after players draw their hands, they don't use the boneyard.

Number of players:	Two to four
What you need:	A twenty-eight-domino deck
Setup:	Divide the dominoes equally among the players so that there are four left over
Object:	To have the fewest pips in your hand at the end of each round
How to play:	

1. The first player puts down the set.

2. This player continues to add dominoes until he or she can't match any more dominoes.

3. Then the next player goes. This player tries to match as many dominoes as possible.

4. Play continues until nobody can match any more dominoes.

5. Each player's score is the pips on the dominoes in his or her hand.

6. More rounds are played. The loser of all the rounds is the first person to reach 100 points.

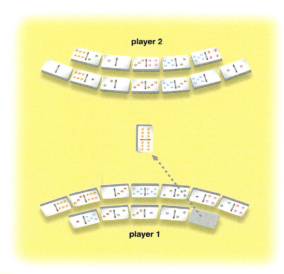

player 2

player 1

▲ *Setup for Hungarian dominoes*

4 dominoes left over

Playing with Dominoes

Children and adults around the world play dominoes. To win domino games, you need skill and luck. To win this game, you also need practice.

You can play other games with dominoes. Try building a house of dominoes. Or set up a line of standing dominoes to show your friends. When your line is set up, push the first domino. It should fall against the next domino in line. One by one, the line of dominoes will fall. There are lots of ways to have fun with dominoes!

▲ *Make up your own domino games!*

Glossary

blank—an end of a domino with no pips

blocked—the state of play when players can't put any dominoes down and can't draw from the boneyard

boneyard—the dominoes left over after players have drawn their hands

deck—a set of dominoes

dominoes—rectangular game pieces marked with dots called pips

double—a domino with the same number of pips on each end

draw—to pick one or more dominoes from the boneyard

ends—the two sides of the front of a domino

face—the side of a domino with dots or blanks on it

hands—the dominoes that players pick from the boneyard

line—the row of dominoes in play faceup on the table

match—to place one end of a domino next to the end of a played domino with the same number of pips

open ends—the ends in the row of dominoes that can be played on

pips—the dots on a domino

set—the first domino played in a game

Did You Know?

If a domino has lots of pips on it, it's called heavy. If a domino has a few pips on it, it's called light.

In Miami, Florida, Cuban-American men play dominoes outdoors.

Some sets have ninety-one dominoes. They are called double-twelve decks.

The boneyard is also called the stock, the kitty, or the reserve.

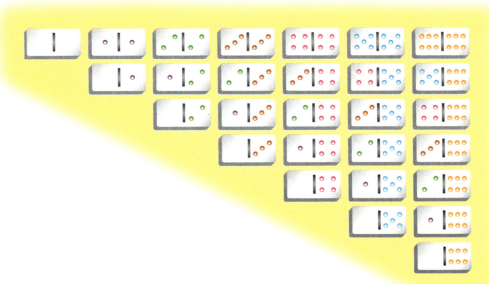

▲ *The twenty-eight–domino deck*

Want to Know More?

At the Library

Berndt, Frederick. *The Domino Book.* Nashville, Tenn.: Thomas Nelson Inc., Publishers, 1974.

Editors of Planet Dexter. *Dominoes.* Reading, Mass.: Addison-Wesley Publishing Company, 1996.

Kelley, Jennifer A. *Great Book of Domino Games.* New York: Sterling Publishing Co., Inc., 1999.

Lankford, Mary D. *Dominoes Around the World.* New York: Morrow Junior Books, 1998.

Muller, Reiner F. *Dominoes: Basic Variations and Rules.* New York: Sterling Publishing Co., Inc., 1995.

On the Web

Board Game Central

http://www.boardgamecentral.com/dominoes/

For an introduction to the game of dominoes and rules for more than ten different games

Dominoes

http://web.ukonline.co.uk/james.masters/TraditionalGames/Dominoes.htm

For a brief history of the game of dominoes

Dominoes Terms and Languages

http://www.gamecabinet.com/rules/DominoTerms.html

For an explanation of many domino terms

Through the Mail

Canadian Children's Museum

at the Canadian Museum of Civilization

100 Laurier Street

Hull, Quebec J8X 4H2

Canada

To write for information about their exhibit with old and new toys and games from around the world

On the Road

Guinness World Records Museum

4943 Clifton Hill

Niagara Falls, Ontario L2G 3N5

Canada

905/356-2299

To see an exhibit of toppling dominoes

Index

About the Author
After graduating from Brown University, Elizabeth Dana Jaffe received her master's degree in early education from Bank Street College of Education. Since then, she has written and edited educational materials. Elizabeth Dana Jaffe lives in New York City.